I0152416

There Is
No Impossible

Diana Calvo Slater

There Is No Impossible
All Rights Reserved.
Copyright © 2023 Diana Calvo Slater
v2.0

The opinions expressed in this manuscript are solely the opinions of the author and do not represent the opinions or thoughts of the publisher. The author has represented and warranted full ownership and/or legal right to publish all the materials in this book.

This book may not be reproduced, transmitted, or stored in whole or in part by any means, including graphic, electronic, or mechanical without the express written consent of the publisher except in the case of brief quotations embodied in critical articles and reviews.

ISBN: 979-8-218-95613-4

Cover Photo © 2023 Diana Calvo Slater and www.gettyimages.com. All rights reserved - used with permission.

CRG Publishing

PRINTED IN THE UNITED STATES OF AMERICA

Table of Contents

CHAPTER 1

Parents

I WAS BORN on Guam, which is a United States territory, on September 27, 1966. I am the youngest of ten children. I have five brothers and four sisters. The age gap between my sisters and I is at least ten years so I didn't have a sister around to ask for advice. My brothers are more than five years older than me. All my siblings left Guam after they graduated from high school.

My mother and father were born in 1923 and 1924 on Guam.

My parents were seventeen and eighteen years old when World War II started and the Japanese invaded Guam. Both my parents were forced to work for the Japanese for only a handful of rice a day. My father walked several miles to work every day. He helped build the airport runway. My mother worked every day on a rice plantation. The war started on December 8, 1941, and ended on July 21, 1944, when the United States military landed and took back the island.

After the war was over my father bought a vehicle that he bid on from a surplus of United States government vehicles.

I have heard two different stories of how my parents met. The first version is that my mother was riding the bus to go to weaving school and my father happened to be on the same bus and that is how they met. The second version is that my father's first cousin was a priest (Pale Scott) and was assigned to the Inarajan church. My father and his other first cousin, Felix, drove from Agana village, where he resided, to Inarajan village, where my mother resided, to help Pale Scott. When they were in Inarajan they visited a small store my grandfather, Tata, and grandmother, Nana, owned. My mother and her sister Laura were working at the store when my father and his first cousin Felix walked into the store. I am not sure how long my parents dated before they got married.

My parents were married in January 1947. My father worked as a mechanic and my mother was a stay-at-home mom. My oldest sibling was born in January 1948. My parents were devout Catholics. The whole family attended Mass every Sunday and all the Holy Days of Obligation. Our first house was near the Catholic Church so the family would walk to church services. Someone once commented to me that when we walked to church it looked like a mother hen with all her baby chicks walking behind her.

My earliest childhood memory about going to church is when I was a child I was attending Mass with my family. I didn't understand the true meaning of the Mass, and most of the time the priest was giving his sermon I didn't know what he was talking about. As a child I attended Mass because I had to, but now prayer is a part of my daily ritual.

Sometime during my elementary school years while I was attending Mass with my parents, the priest was talking about the Lamb of God. I looked up on the altar and saw a picture of a lamb. I initially thought that the Lamb of God was an actual pet lamb that belonged to God. Sometime later, during Sunday school, my teacher explained to the class the meaning of the Lamb of God. After that lesson I felt like I had one of those dumb moments.

My father was a simple, proud man who worked hard. He was always very serious and strict. He did not have a sense of humor. I am not sure if it was because he had to be responsible for a big family or if that was just the way he was. At one point my father worked several jobs to support the family. Most of his life he worked as an auto mechanic for the United States federal government. He came home from work with grease under his fingernails. He spent quite a while washing his hands and scrubbing the grease out.

Whenever he needed a vehicle he would buy surplus vehicles with minor problems from the U.S. government and was always able to fix the problem to make the car run smoothly. He was in his seventies when he bought his first and only new car. He was very proud to have a new car.

My father did not have any hobbies or a group of friends that he spent time with. Once in a while my uncles, his brothers, came to our house or he went to their houses. They would reminisce about old times while drinking Johnny Walker Blue Label. That was the only time that I saw my father drink alcohol. He was always happy after he spent time with his brothers.

He would drink coffee with my mother every morning and read the newspaper. He enjoyed watching television in the evenings. We had one television set, approximately fifteen inches big, with rabbit ears and no remote control. When my father wanted the channel changed I had to sit in front of the television set and turn the dial. He enjoyed watching The Rockford Files, The Streets of San Francisco and The Price is Right. He did the grocery shopping. Some of the groceries he bought were canned foods that included Spam, corned beef, Vienna sausage, and potted meat. He also bought fresh bread, meats, and vegetables. He would often tell me the story that he remembered when a loaf of bread was ten cents. He also enjoyed eating sweets. He bought apple turnovers at least once a week and ate them with his coffee. He bought hopscotch ice cream, which is basically a mixture of vanilla and chocolate. That was the only flavor ice cream I had for many years.

The family did not drink tap water because it was considered unsafe. My father collected rainwater in a fifty-five gallon metal drum covered with a steel screen. After he collected the rainwater in a pitcher, he placed it in a pot on the stove and boiled it, let it cool down, and then placed it in the refrigerator. I never drank plain water growing up because I still tasted the metal in my mouth. I always added Tang or Kool-Aid to mask the taste.

My father never allowed me to have friends come to our house. I wasn't allowed to go on any dates and was rarely allowed to receive telephone calls. A few times I received telephone calls from my friends, but I had a time limit on the phone. My sisters went on dates but they always had to bring me along. My sisters are between ten years to sixteen years older than me. I never asked my father why he never allowed me to go out on dates.

My father was not an affectionate man and he was a man of few words. I am not sure if he was proud of me, but I sure hope he was. From what I can remember I was a good child who did what I was supposed to do.

When I introduced my father to my first future husband, he told me he did not want me to get married to him. I was under the impression that he did not like him, although he never came out and told me. Robert was younger than me and did not have a college education. I think my father wanted someone to take care of me, and to him it seemed like Robert was not capable of doing that.

When I introduced my father to my second husband, he was happy. Roger and I have an eighteen-year age gap, and I was surprised that my father did not mention anything about it. He was always very respectful toward Roger. I think it had a lot to do with the fact that Roger was a successful business man and was capable of taking care of me.

My father was diagnosed with dementia when he was in his eighties. I was with him when the doctor gave him the news, and he got very upset with the doctor. I was concerned because that was the first time I had seen my father so upset. I realized that if my father could not get to his bank account, it would be a good idea that I should also be a signer on his account, and he agreed. My father and I went to the bank to meet with a banker and sign the documents. I was glad I did it, because there were many occasions when I had to withdraw money to help care for my parents.

On several occasions my father would go grocery shopping and forget where he parked his car. I was a passenger when my father was driving, and he became aggressive. He started speeding and following cars too closely. He was always a good driver before he was diagnosed with dementia. I worried that something bad could happen every time my father drove.

I called my older sister in California and told her of what had transpired with our father's driving. She decided to come to Guam to visit our parents. My sister and I were concerned that our father might hurt someone with his vehicle. We came up with a plan regarding our father's car. My sister borrowed his car, drove it to my house, and parked it there. When she arrived back at our parents' house she told our father that she parked the car in a parking lot and when she tried to get back to the car, she discovered that it was stolen. We took his car to a car dealership and sold the car. We used the money from the sale of his car for my parents. After the car was gone my sister told me that our father went outside to his garage every day and stated, "I know Marie and Diana stole my car." That broke my heart, but we had to do what was best for him.

In the later stages of my father's dementia it was extremely difficult to see my father deteriorate. He was once a proud, hardworking man, but he turned into a child, and it still makes me cry.

The day before I was to leave on a trip for my daughter's wedding in California, I had a strange feeling that I needed to see my father before I left, because it might be my last time. I walked into my parents' house and my father was sitting in a wheelchair. I sat next to him and talked to him. He didn't recognize me and he just stared straight ahead. I told him I loved him and kissed him on the forehead. A couple days later my sister-in-law called me from Guam to tell me the sad news that Dad had passed away. I was sad and cried, but I was grateful to see him one last time and tell him that I loved him.

My mother was a stay-at-home mom with many talents. We didn't have a washing machine for many years. She washed all the clothes by hand in a rectangular concrete sink approximately four feet long. After washing all the clothes she hung them on a clothesline. As I got older we had a washing machine with a ringer, but we never had a dryer. My mother told me when she was a child she would take all the clothes to the river to wash them. It took an entire day to wash all the family's clothes.

She did the cooking and never used a cookbook. I remember asking her for a recipe, and she just recited it by memory. Some of the meals she cooked included fried fish, fried chicken, oxtail and mongo beans, pig's feet, various hamburger dishes, and a variety of soups. My all-time favorite dish is escabeche, which consists of fried fish, various types of vegetables, and turmeric. Some of my favorites that she made were pumpkin turnovers, lemai (breadfruit) donuts, banana donuts, and yeast donuts. She would roll her yeast donuts and let it rise on the kitchen table. She fried the donuts, and when the donuts were cooked she placed them in a brown paper bag filled with sugar and cinnamon and shook the bag. The smell and taste of the warm fresh donuts were amazing.

She had an amazing green thumb. The front and backyards of our house were filled with various plants that she had planted. She planted flowers, mango trees, avocado trees, breadfruit trees, guava trees, star apple trees, pomegranate trees, and a macadamia nut tree. She was extremely proud of all her plants.

My mother was not afraid of anything except snakes. Several times she was attending to her garden when she saw a snake and screamed. My father came outside with his machete and killed the snake, even though the snakes on Guam are not poisonous.

She also had a sewing machine and sewed all her clothes. When I was young she asked me if I wanted to learn to sew, but I told her I wasn't interested in learning. I regretted not learning to sew.

She loved to weave, mostly mats. The process of weaving mats is very lengthy. She picked the leaves off the pandanas plants in our yard, boiled the leaves, and then dried them out in the sun. After drying out the leaves she would start weaving. Over the years my husband bought several mats from my mother. For years we placed the mats on our living room floor. Every time I walked into our living room it reminded me of my mother.

My parents usually spoke to me in Chamorro, the native language of Guam, but I always answered them in English. I tried to learn Chamorro as a young child, but a family member made fun of me, and I was discouraged.

My mother was a woman of few words, but she had many talents. My mother's father, Tata, passed away before I was born. I asked her what Tata was like. She told me that Tata was an alcoholic and physically abused my grandmother, Nana. After that response I never brought up the subject of Tata.

As a young child my mother was also known as Cinderella. I asked one of my relatives how she had gotten that nickname. According to the relatives, she was beautiful when she was young and had many admirers. She always took pride in her figure. When I was growing up she constantly reminded me that her waist was eighteen inches.

We didn't have any mother-and-daughter talks. We did not have a good or close relationship. The only advice she gave me when I was growing up was to be careful when crossing the street and to look both ways. I was always trying to find ways to make my mother proud of me. I had a weight issue for most of my life. I was a chunky child. My mother constantly told me that I was fat and needed to lose weight.

My sisters told me that our mother was different and not critical with them. I am not sure if it was because my mother had me at the age of forty-three that she was so critical. A lot of times when I was growing up it seemed that whatever I did was not good enough for her, and it would go back to my weight issues. I was constantly trying to get her approval.

My mother was not an affectionate person, and it probably has a lot to do with when she grew up. Her parents', my grandparents', generation didn't show any kind of affection toward her or any of her siblings. My parents did their best to raise me and my siblings.

In 1992 my mother was diagnosed with colon cancer. The doctor told the family that she had six months to live. I was scared for my mother and for the rest of the family. I know that we were never close, but she was still my mother, and I was not ready for her to go yet. I wanted to be able to spend more time with her and for her to get to know my children. She recovered and lived for many, many more years. It goes to show that doctors are not God. Only God knows how long we are here for.

My mother had always been the type of person that spoke her mind with no filters.

My happiest memory of my mother was when she had her eightieth birthday. Several months before her birthday I wanted to have a surprise party for my mother. My goal was to get all my siblings to come back to Guam for her birthday; however I was not successful. A total of four of the children attended my mother's birthday party. On the day of the party the decorations were put up and the tables were set and my mother was all smiles while walking around the house. I had never seen my mother that happy in many years. She said, "I know this party is for me."I was happy because I succeeded in making her happy.

A few years later she was diagnosed with dementia. I had never imagined that any of my family, let alone my mother, would have dementia. I felt like the inside of my body was torn up. I wanted to be strong for my parents, but sometimes I would sit and cry. As the dementia progressed she became like a child again, and I felt extremely sad and helpless. The mother I knew when I was growing up was not there anymore. She passed away in her sleep. I never got to say goodbye or tell her I loved her one last time. To this day I regret not being there toward the end; however, I try to focus on the good times, especially her eightieth birthday party.

CHAPTER 2

My Education

Elementary School

WHEN I WAS born our family lived in Ordot, Guam. I am the youngest of ten children. I have very vague memories as a child, and some of them are not happy. One of my sisters told me that they gave me a baby chick to hold in my hands and I squeezed it and it died. I don't remember that, but I must have been excited to be holding a baby chick. My first traumatic memory was when I was sexually assaulted as a young child by a close relative. I was sitting on his lap and he touched my private area, my vagina. I can't remember if there was anyone else there at the time the incident occurred. That same relative called me an ugly duckling when I was about five or six years old.

I was four or five years old when we moved to a new concrete house in Mongmong. The house had three bedrooms and one and a half bathrooms. One bedroom was my parents' room, one bedroom was the boys' room, and the other room was the girls' room. The back of the house had a tin roof where my father put a clothesline and a washing machine so my mother could hang the clean clothes up after they were washed.

I don't remember my first day of kindergarten, but my mother told me that when she took me to the bus stop I cried and did not want to get on the bus. When I was in the fifth grade I started wearing a training bra. I was sitting in the classroom and the boy sitting behind me pulled the back of my bra strap. I turned around and told him to stop. I was also in the fifth grade when I started playing volleyball in school, and I really enjoyed that. Playing volleyball made me feel happy and that helped me divert my attention from my problems.

I had two good friends in elementary school named Mary and Nina. Mary told me that her father was very strict when it came to disciplining her and her siblings. One day Mary's brother came to school with his head shaved, and I asked her what happened to her brother. Mary told me that her brother did something bad and her father shaved her brother's head. I felt bad for her brother.

During my elementary years I enjoyed playing jacks and hopscotch. I had a ball and jacks that I would play with outside. Hopscotch is a game where we would take a piece of chalk and draw squares on the concrete and write numbers in the squares. The person would then take a small rock and start on square number one. It involved hopping from one square to another. Playing jacks and hopscotch always made me happy. I also had a doll that I received as a gift that I enjoyed playing with. Our family did not have much money, but we always had food to eat. We didn't have turkey on Thanksgiving or a Christmas tree during the holidays. We ate chicken on Thanksgiving and Christmas dinner wasn't fancy either.

My father had a loud speaker situated on the roof of our garage and a microphone inside the house. He used it to call me or my siblings if we were not home by a certain time. All the neighbors definitely knew all our names, and at first it was embarrassing, but we got used to it. If my siblings or I were ever up to something no good, my father would just stare and give us a mean look. We knew if we didn't get our act together we would get a whipping, usually with the belt.

We had a lot of chickens that roamed around our yard, and my father fed them. He bought a huge bag of hen scratch for the chickens. When the hen laid eggs he collected them and we would eat the eggs. Sometime during my elementary school years my father was at the back of the house. I saw my father pick up a chicken, fling it around, and snap its neck. I was traumatized. I asked him what he was going to do with the chicken. My father said, "I am going to pluck the feathers, boil it, and it will be our dinner." I told him that I am not eating that chicken and that I will eat Spam or Vienna sausage. He looked at me and said, "You eat the chicken that I buy at the grocery store."

I said, "Yes, but I didn't see that chicken die."

There was also another time when we had a pig in a cage at the back of the house. At the time I didn't realize that my father was feeding the pig to fatten it up for the sole purpose of killing it for a party. The day that my father and other family members killed that pig was horrible. I did not see the pig when they were killing it, but the sound of the squeal was deafening. I felt so sorry for the pig that I was crying. I have always been an animal lover, and I can't stand it when an animal is killed.

When I was eleven one my brothers took a lead pencil and stabbed the palm of my right hand. The lead did not go into my skin but the scar is still on my hand. I don't remember what happened that would make my brother angry with me.

I have been cleaning house since as far back as I can remember. I used to joke that I have been cleaning since I crawled out of the playpen. I would clean the bathrooms, sweep, mop, and dust. The sweeping and mopping would be done daily. My mother cooked and did all the laundry. All the windows had metal louvers with screen on the outside. We had a couple of fans that were placed on the floor, but we didn't have any air conditioning in the house.

My mother told me almost daily that I was fat and needed to lose weight. I never understood why my mother was so critical about my weight. She would often tell me the story of how when she was growing up her waist was eighteen inches. Looking back now I don't think my mother intentionally meant to hurt me, but she did. Emotional abuse can stay with you for life.

I started feeling occasional bouts of sadness in the fifth grade. Most of the time school was the only place where I was happy.

Middle School

I attended Untalan Junior High from sixth grade to the eighth grade. I was not involved in any sports or extracurricular activities. I basically went to school and came home and did my chores.

The only advice I received from my mother when I was growing up was "Be careful when you cross the street." I was eleven when I had my first menstrual cycle in junior high school. My mother did not tell me about becoming a woman. I thought I was dying and didn't understand why I was bleeding. I went to my mother crying, and she started laughing at me. She said, "You are not dying, you have your period." I never understood why my mother did not explain things about life instead of laughing at me.

Sometime during junior high school a girl was teasing me in school, but I don't know what she was teasing me about. I was upset and ended up on the ground rolling around with her. My classmates broke up the fight. That was the first time I was so upset over someone teasing me that I ended up fighting with them. All those years I kept all my feelings bottled up inside, and it just exploded.

I started experimenting with baking boxed cakes in junior high school. I baked the cakes for the family. One day I made Rice Crispy treats and brought them to school, and my friends loved them. The feeling of being appreciated and people happy with my treats made me happy too. Every time we had some kind of party in school my friends asked me to make Rice Crispy treats.

My classmates and I decided to participate in a walk-a-thon. It was twenty-six miles, which was basically from one end of the island to the other end. I did not do any kind of preparation to prepare myself for the walk-a-thon. I don't think I thought the whole thing through. It took me all day to complete the walk-a-thon, but I was extremely proud that I finished. The next day I was so sore I could barely walk. I learned that the next time I was going to participate in any kind of physical activity I should take baby steps and not overdo it.

My home life was not terrible but I always felt like my mother was never happy with me. My weight continued to increase and my thighs started rubbing together. I constantly had rash on my thighs and had to put on baby powder to heal it. Almost on a daily basis my mother told me that I was fat and needed to lose weight. She would reminisce about her eighteen-inch waist and comment that she was never fat. There were times when I was depressed about my weight and thought if I was thin I would be happy.

My parents did not allow me to have any friends at our house. I was definitely not allowed to have any boyfriends. In junior high a boy liked me for the first time, and he asked me to be his girlfriend. I was happy because I never thought any boy would find me attractive. We went steady for a few months and then he broke up with me. He told me the reason he wanted to break up was because I was too fat. My heart was broken and thought no one would ever want to be with me because of my weight problem. My friends were all thin, and I felt that nobody could understand how I felt.

My friends' parents allowed them to attend outside activities to include going to the movies, roller skating, and going to parties. My father allowed me to attend these activities with friends; however, he had to be present too. On one occasion my friends and I met at the roller skating rink, and of course my father was there. While I was skating around the rink a boy started skating near me, and my father became upset. After that incident I was embarrassed and told my father I wanted to go home. I felt like I could never fit in with my friends because my father always had to be with us. My mother made me feel like I would be looked at differently because I was overweight. My father made me feel like I was being suffocated. I could never fit in with my friends. I was feeling depressed more often. I sometimes felt like I didn't want to live anymore, or it would have been better if I was never born.

High School

I attended George Washington High School from ninth to eleventh grades. My parents and I left Guam after the end of my junior year. We moved to California to live with my sister and brother-in-law. I attended Highlands High School during my senior year.

During my high school years my days basically involved going to school and coming home. My father did not allow me to join any sport or school activity. Sometimes I felt like I was always confined. Nobody at school ever said anything to me about my weight until one day one of my classmates called me thunder thighs. I went home that day and cried. They say that words never hurt is so untrue. I still remember the thunder-thighs comment like it was just yesterday. Emotional abuse can stay with a person forever. To this date I still have a hard time dealing with any kind of criticism about my body.

During my senior year in high school I was in a new school, and I felt like I didn't belong. I made one friend, and I was grateful. I felt like my friend really understood me. I really wanted to go to my senior prom; however, no one asked me. Anyway, if by chance anyone asked me to go to the prom, my father would have attended the prom with me. It seemed that boys were not interested in me.

The best thing about my high school years was living with my sister. I have always looked up to her and felt that she always had life figured out. I always admired all my sisters. Growing up I sometimes felt like Cinderella because I was always cleaning and felt like I didn't belong in the family. My sisters told me when they were young they were allowed to go on dates, but they had to bring me along.

I definitely think that seeing a counselor or therapist would have benefited me. I didn't know it then but it was God who helped me through all my school years.

After my high school graduation my parents moved back to Guam. I continued to live with my sister, and I started college at the university. My father wanted me to become an accountant. I was struggling with all my classes in college, especially accounting and economics. I was getting mostly D grades. I realized that I did not want to be an accountant and I was doing it only to make my father happy. I ended up dropping out of college and felt like a failure.

Depression began to set in again. I didn't know what I wanted to do as a career. I wished I was one of those people who knew early in life what they wanted to do. Deep inside I wanted to be like my sister

Lourdes. She graduated from high school as the valedictorian, went on to college, and became a pharmacist.

After I dropped out of college I lived in California with a couple of my sisters for a few years. I worked as a cashier and waitress to earn money. In 1988 I decided to move back to Guam hoping I would be able to figure my life out.

I moved back in with my parents because I did not have enough money saved up to live on my own. I worked as a cashier during the day and waitress at night. I was living in my parents' garage, which was converted into a bedroom. For the first time in my adult life I felt like I had some privacy.

After working for several months I still wasn't motivated in choosing a career path. I was beginning to think that I was the type of person who never decides on a career and keeps going from job to job.

Late 1988 I was walking around doing some window shopping at the local shopping center on Guam when I was approached by a female adult. The female told me that I was pretty and that she was involved in the local beauty pageant. She asked me if I was interested in join-ing the beauty pageant. I don't remember what my response was, but I do know that I was one of the contestants. I was nowhere near ready and had some lower body fat to lose, but I fell for the pretty compliment. Up until then I hardly received any nice compliments from anyone. I didn't win the competition, but it sure helped me build up my confidence.

CHAPTER 3

First Husband

I MET MY first husband sometime in the year 1989 at a dance club. I didn't want to go out, but my good friend convinced me to go. I was sitting down with my friend and a good looking man asked me to dance. He asked for my phone number, and we went on our first date. I was flattered because it was the first time a good-looking man with a nice body was interested in me. I started to have self-confidence, and it felt great. He told me that he would rather spend time with me than with his friends. I fell in love. We dated for several months before we got married.

We got married in February 1990. We lived with his mother and step-father for several months. My in-laws had a catering business. The employees at the catering business worked six days a week and long hours. I was overworked to the point that I had chest pains and thought I was having a heart attack. The ambulance took me to the emergency room at the hospital. I was so scared of the thought of dying. I wasn't ready. I knew that I had so much more life to live. The doctor saw me and told me that I had an anxiety attack. I felt so stupid. At that point I told myself I wasn't going to overwork myself again and I would try to relax.

My first husband and I decided to move to Southern California some-time later in 1990. We rented an apartment, and that was the first time we were actually alone. We really got to know each other, and our relationship was great. During March 1991 we found out that I was pregnant. I was super excited and prayed that I would have a healthy baby. I would listen to music to relax when I wasn't working. Sometimes I put the headphones over my belly and played the music for my baby. During my pregnancy my first husband occasionally stayed out late. He had a part-time job at night at a pool hall. After the pool hall closed he would stay and play pool with his friends. I woke up one morning at four a.m. and realized he wasn't home. I drove to the pool hall and found him there with his friends. I was so angry that I pounded on the door. I asked him to stop making me worry by staying out late. He told me that I was overreacting and that it was my pregnancy hormones.

During my pregnancy most people did not realize that I was pregnant. The comment I would get from most people was, "I didn't know that you were pregnant. I thought you were just fat." I cried when I heard that comment.

I had a fifteen-hour labor, but it was all worth the pain when I saw my daughter. Childbirth is the most amazing experience. Holding my daughter for the first time was awesome. Being a mother is the greatest accomplishment. The wonderful smell of a baby was something I enjoyed every day. I breast fed her for twelve months. Watching your child experience everything for the first time is beyond what words can describe.

We moved back to Guam during the summer of 1992. At first we were renting a house and then later moved into an apartment. My first husband and I started having marital problems toward the end of the year. We argued most of the time.

I stopped breastfeeding sometime during December 1992. As soon as I stopped breastfeeding I found out I was pregnant again. When

I went to the doctor he told me that my estimated date of delivery was in September 1993. When I found out I was pregnant I had many different emotions, especially because we were having marital problems.

During my second pregnancy my first husband often went out with his friends or to nightclubs. Having my daughter with me when I was pregnant was very comforting, especially because I felt that my first husband wasn't around enough.

I was having contractions and started bleeding in July 1993, so we went to the hospital emergency room. I felt a lot of pain, and I was afraid for my baby. I waited for several minutes before the hospital personnel checked me in. The doctor told me that the baby was too early for natural childbirth and that I would have to have a cesarean. The anesthesia that was given to me while in the operating room did not work. I felt all the pain, and I tried to scream but was not able to. My son was born two months early and weighed three pounds and eight ounces. He wasn't able to breathe on his own for several days, so the hospital put him on a ventilator. He stayed in the hospital for five weeks. I was heartbroken and felt empty because I couldn't take him home for several weeks. I went to the hospital every day to see him and tried to breastfeed him. For some reason I was unable to produce any breast milk, and that made me feel even more like a failure as a new mother. I felt as if I did not bond with my son because I was not able to breastfeed him. After five weeks, which seemed like an eternity, I finally brought my son home. Having a daughter and a son made me feel complete as a mother. I always wanted one girl and one boy, and I thanked God I had healthy children. Both my children always slept through the night and were always great.

My husband's and my marital problems had gotten to the point that the marriage was beyond saving. My first husband became involved in drugs, methamphetamines. He would not come home for days.

He wouldn't call to say where he was, and I worried sick. All sorts of bad thoughts crossed my mind because I didn't know where he was. When he finally came home he was angry. The last time he came home from being gone for one week he was furious. He placed his hands around my neck and started choking me. I decided at that moment that I did not want my children growing up thinking that this behavior was the norm. I grew up with emotional and sexual abuse. I didn't want my children to experience any kind of abuse. I took my children and our belongings and left the apartment.

Although I would have preferred to live on my own with my children, I could not afford it. It was the later part of 1996 when we moved back into my parents' house. We were living in the bedroom that was initially a garage that was converted into a bedroom. We had to go to the main house to eat and use the restroom. I worked full time and paid for my bills, which included my car payment. I also paid for a sitter for my children. I did not want to burden my parents to take care of my children, because they were elderly. When I wasn't working and taking care of my children, I started to have thoughts of depression and failure once again. I cried a lot. I prayed and asked God to send me a man who would treat me like a queen and accept my children like his own. My daughter was four years old and my son was three years old at that time.

One night my daughter climbed on my lap and said, "Mommy can you buy me a daddy that would spend time with us?" I started crying and told her I wished I was able to do it, but I couldn't. She knew that her biological father was hardly ever around for them.

Riacca and Franco were always well behaved until we were living at my parents' house. I think they were probably acting out because I was no longer with their biological father. All three incidents happened when I was sleeping. I woke up on three separate occasions to find the children had gotten into mischief. There was the lotion episode, the powder episode, and the lipstick episode. One morning I woke up and Riacca had put lotion all over Franco's hair. I asked her what was she doing, and she didn't have any response. Needless to say it took a while to wash all the lotion out of his hair. The morning I woke up and there was baby powder all over the room. Riacca said she wanted it to snow. The last episode was the lipstick. I woke up to find that Riacca had a towel covering her face and body. I asked her to remove the towel, please. After she removed the towel I saw that she had lipstick all over her face. Her explanation was priceless. "I wanted to wear lipstick like you, Mommy." After the three incidents the children were angels again.

When I felt depressed, instead of turning to food for comfort I turned to exercise. I started jogging and began to lose weight. I was receiving compliments from different people and for the first time in a long time started to feel good about myself.

It was stressful having to live at my parents' house. Being back home brought back a lot of traumatic memories. Whenever my mind started to flashback to those memories, I would say extra prayers.

I started a diet that included only bread and butter. Bread is my favorite carbohydrate, and of course butter goes best with bread. I wasn't getting anywhere with further weight loss, so I decided to try another diet. I started a coffee diet. I would drink only coffee with cream and sugar. The coffee would curb my appetite and I wasn't hungry. I was on the coffee diet for several months.

CHAPTER 4

Second Husband

IN THE YEAR 1997 I was working as a sales associate at a high-end boutique. The customers that frequented the boutique were mostly Japanese tourists. I only went to work, went jogging, or was home with my children. Sometime in the end of August 1998 my manager at the time told me he had a friend who wanted to take me out on a date. I asked my manager, "Where did your friend see me? Was it at work or was I jogging? I said to him, "Did your friend see me jogging and stop to talk to me?"

My manager said, "No."

I said, "Okay, let me have your friend's number."

Two weeks later my manager gave me a piece of paper with the name Roger and a phone number. I called Roger, and he asked me to meet him for lunch at a Japanese restaurant in the Hilton Hotel. We met for lunch and ended up talking for several hours and got to know each other. I was so nervous that my palms were sweaty. I had never had a date with a sophisticated older man.

After lunch I went to work, and Roger sent me a text message. I called Roger, and he invited my children and me to brunch at his house. I felt like I was walking on a cloud and that God had answered my prayer.

The children and I arrived at Roger's house for brunch and he introduced me to CJ, Roger's son from his first marriage. CJ was thirteen at the time. Roger cooked for all of us and even made a birthday cake for me. That was the first time anyone had baked a cake for me. I felt so special that day.

I wanted to find a man with a good heart and not just good looks. I believe if you have a good heart you will always have a good heart. The children and I moved in with Roger and CJ. CJ was always good to my children. Roger accepted my children and treated them just like his own. His treatment of my children made me fall more in love with him. A man who was willing to accept the package deal, my children and me, is definitely hard to find.

I quit my job at the high-end boutique and focused on spending time with the children. I realized I was very fortunate to have that precious time with the children. I also adopted our first cat from the animal shelter. I named him Cupid. Some weeks later I noticed an outside cat that came to the window, and Cupid would touch the window as if he wanted to play with him. I decided Cupid needed a friend, and I was right. I named our second cat Sammy. They played together like two brothers. I always enjoyed watching them together.

We got engaged in late 1998, and we were married in June 1999 in a Catholic church. All three of the children had roles in the wedding. CJ was the best man, Riacca was the flower girl, and Franco was the ring bearer. I did not show Riacca how to properly toss the flowers at the wedding and she ended up throwing them in an antagonistic way. The way she threw the flowers made me laugh. We had an intimate wedding and reception that included mostly family and friends. Everyone had a great time. About a week later we left for our honeymoon in Cancun, Mexico. The honeymoon was very relaxing.

CHAPTER 5

Children

I MET CJ when he was thirteen years old, and he was always very respectful toward me. At first he called me Miss Diana, but I asked him to call me just Diana. CJ always excelled in school. According to Roger at about the age of twelve CJ knew he wanted to go into submarines. He was also an Eagle Scout in the boy scouts. In high school he played football. CJ received the Most Inspirational Player trophy all three years that he was at Father Duenas High School. During his football games I would bake a huge batch of chocolate chip cookies. The boys loved the cookies, and they sure went pretty quickly. One of his teammates stacked up the cookies so high it reminded me of a can of Pringles chips.

CJ graduated from high school and went on to attend and graduate from the United States Naval Academy. He served five years in the United States Navy as an officer. He is happily married and has three beautiful children.

I was fortunate that I was able to be a stay-at-home mom while my children were young. I enjoyed spending time with them and watching them grow. I dropped them off and picked them up from school every day. I took them to all their games and extracurricular activities. I wanted my children to enjoy the carefree life of being a child.

I would tell them that their only job was to do their best in school. I always prayed that my children would be happy and successful in school and in life.

Riacca was always a happy baby and never fussed. Sometime in 1996, when Riacca was four years old, she swallowed a quarter. I was so frightened that I drove straight to the doctor's office and told the doctor what happened. X-rays were taken of her chest and at first they couldn't see the image of the quarter in her chest. When they finally discovered where the quarter was, she was rushed to the hospital. The doctor had to perform an operation to extract the quarter. The doctor told me that he would not have to cut an incision and would use an instrument placed down her throat to extract the quarter. After the procedure I stayed at the hospital with Riacca and thanked God she was okay.

Riacca has always been independent, even as a little girl. She started kindergarten at the age of four. On her first day of school she walked right into the classroom, sat down, and said, "Bye, Mommy." She didn't even cry. She always did her schoolwork without me reminding her. She always had good grades.

She started playing sports in middle school to include flag rugby, volleyball, soccer, and basketball. I think her favorite sport is rugby. When she was eleven years old, after one of her basketball practices her coach brought her home. I answered the door and she was holding up her left hand. Her coach told me she probably broke a couple of her fingers. I was scared but remained calm.

I asked Riacca if she was okay.

Riacca was so tough she wasn't even crying. She said to me, "Mom, it's my wedding finger."

I replied, "You are eleven, and that is still far way."

I took Riacca to an urgent care center, and the doctor said that she broke two fingers and one of the broken fingers was also dislocated.

In high school she continued to play sports, including football. She was the first and only girl who played on the high school football team. I was so proud of her and I was also scared because I did not want her to get hurt. There was always a group of spectators that cheered for her every time she went onto the football field.

She was involved in extracurricular activities to include the being in the National Honor Society, being president of Youth for Youth, acting as an altar server at church, and being a volunteer for the Salvation Army. She has always been very driven.

In the year 2006 we all attended CJ's graduation and commissioning from the United States Naval Academy. It was a beautiful campus and the chapel was breathtaking. While we were walking around the campus Riacca said, "I think I want to go here too."

Roger helped Riacca start the process of applying to the Naval Academy. Riacca graduated from high school in 2009. She attended the Naval Academy Prep School for one year and then went on to attend the United States Naval Academy. She played four years of tackle rugby at the Naval Academy. While she was playing rugby she broke her ankle and had to wear a boot for a while. She was one tough cookie. She graduated from the Naval Academy in 2014 and was commissioned as a United States Marine Corps officer.

Whenever Riacca decided to accomplish a goal she just set her mind to it and put 100 percent into it. She would say, "I learned it from you, Mom."

I always taught my children that they could accomplish anything they set their mind to, as long as they were not afraid of hard work. I believe everyone has the drive and determination embedded in them, but for most people it remains dormant. Only a handful of people find the passion that drives them.

Riacca still plays rugby, but now it is touch, not tackle. I have always enjoyed watching her play all the sports she was involved in. She is married to a wonderful man and she has great in-laws too.

Franco was born two months premature. He was three pounds and eight ounces and his lungs were not fully developed. He was in an incubator and was on a breathing apparatus for several days. He stayed in the hospital for five weeks. I went to the hospital everyday to see him. For some reason I was unable to produce any milk to breastfeed him, which made me feel like an inadequate mother. It seemed like an eternity before I was able to bring him home from the hospital. After I brought him home he was always a good baby, including sleeping through the night.

On his first day of school he was full of tears. He cried when I walked him into the classroom and didn't want me to leave. Of course I cried because I felt bad for leaving him. He eventually got used to going to school. At the age of five he was diagnosed with Attention Deficit Hyperactive Disorder (ADHD) and Pervasive Developmental Disorder (PDD). Initially he had a harder time with schoolwork, but as time passed and with the help of a one-to-one aide his grades improved. There was a time when a part of me blamed myself because I thought if I didn't have Franco prematurely he might not have his disabilities. Franco was always shy and had a hard time making friends. Because of his disabilities he was having problems socializing. For the first several years of elementary school he would only eat Vienna sausages and did not want to try any other type of food. Eventually he went on to try other types of food. During middle school he attended a smaller school, which was better because he had more one-to-one time with the instructor.

Franco was never into sports, but Roger convinced him to join the high school football team. He played for one year and received the Most Inspirational trophy. I asked him if he wanted to play the following year, but he was not interested. His grades in high school were good. He was also involved in extracurricular activities to include Youth for Youth (Nonprofit organization) and altar server at church.

After graduating from high school he attended the Guam Community College. He received an associate of arts degree and a certificate in culinary cooking. He spent a few years working in a couple of different restaurants; however, it was not what he expected it to be. He has grown into a responsible man. I have mentioned to Franco many times that I believe he has drive and determination; he just has to find his passion. I told him I believe he can accomplish anything as long as he sets his mind to it and is not afraid of hard work.

I am extremely proud of my children and all their accomplishments. I continue to pray for them to be safe, healthy, happy, and successful in life.

CHAPTER 6

Exercise/Baking

EVEN AFTER I got married to Roger I continued to go jogging. I decided to go on a fruit diet. I ate only fruit and couldn't figure out why I wasn't losing body fat on my lower body. I'm not sure what I was thinking at the time. It wasn't until sometime later that I learned fruit is full of sugar and the body does not know the difference between naturally sweetened or artificially sweetened food. I also learned that in order to lose weight people have to burn off more calories than they consume.

I started baking mostly cookies and cakes. Sometimes I baked for my family and sometimes I baked and gave it away. I liked seeing people smile when they received my baked goods. Their smile made me smile. I always enjoyed giving more than receiving. I give out of the goodness of my heart and never expect anything in return. To me true giving is never expecting anything in return.

BODYBUILDING

Sometime in December 2000 Roger received a gift certificate for a one-month gym membership at Gold's Gym. He didn't want to use it, so I decided I was going to use the gift certificate. I had never lifted weights and wanted to know more about bodybuilding. I walked into the gym and asked to speak to the general manager. The employee walked me to Joe's office, and I introduced myself and sat down. I mentioned to Joe that I wanted to learn about bodybuilding. Joe stated, "There is the Guam National competition in March 2001." Any normal person would have said, "No thank you, I have no desire to compete," but not me. I responded with, "Am I too late?" To this date I don't why I said that.

Joe introduced me to Terry Debold, a personal trainer. Terry was my personal trainer for the next several months. Terry put me on a workout plan and meal plan. I was doing two hours of cardio every day and resistance training five days a week. The meal plan was very strict, and it included fiber, lean protein with no seasoning, and no carbohydrates. My meals were pretty much the same every day. Breakfast was protein power mixed with water. Lunch was canned tuna rinsed in water, broccoli or a sweet potato steamed with no seasoning. Dinner was protein powder mixed with water. I was allowed to drink only water. The resistance training was extremely difficult; however, the diet was even more difficult for me. I really like eating carbohydrates, including bread and sweets, and most especially chocolate. The lack of carbohydrates made me irritable. Some days I felt like giving up and said to Roger, "What am I trying to prove by competing? I have young children." With the grace of God I was somehow able to make it through the months of training, and I participated in the competition. I won second place, and it was an amazing feeling. That feeling of accomplishment all started with, "Am I too late?" A few weeks later several people asked me if I was going to compete again. I was flattered and said to myself, "Why not?"

During the whole time I was training for the competition I continued to bake and give the baked goods away. Roger enjoyed being my taste tester, because I was on a strict diet, so I could not eat anything that was not on my meal plan. Roger would say, "It's great work if you could get it." Not only did I enjoy baking but it was also my stress reliever.

The next competition was in July 2002. This time I had a different personal trainer, Dave Slagle. Dave was even harder on me than Terry; however, Dave was very encouraging. Dave was a very nice guy. Once again I was on a strict meal plan and workout plan, but this time around I was okay with it, because I knew what to expect. I was prepared to work even harder for my second competition. The resistance training for me that was the most difficult was leg day. Dave would train me so hard that by the next day and sometimes several days after that I had a hard time walking, most especially going up and down stairs.

For the most part when I was dieting I was okay until I smelled food. One of my favorite foods is French fries, but of course I had to give them up while training. One day I went through the drive through at McDonald's to get my children Happy Meals. I handed the food to my children in the back seat. Suddenly the overwhelming smell of French fries overcame me, and I really wanted a French fry. I asked my daughter for one fry and she said, "No, mommy, you can't eat that."

All of a sudden the sound of my voice changed and I demanded, "Give me one fry!" My daughter quickly handed me one fry, and to me it tasted like the first French fry I had ever eaten. It was super good. I apologized to my daughter and tried to explain to her that when I don't have carbohydrates I become a crazy person.

We had dinner at a restaurant once a week as a family. I brought my protein drink in my shaker cup because it was my last meal of the day. I was okay with the fact that the rest of the family ate their dinners while I just had my protein drink. The waitress would take our orders, and when it came time for me to order, I told her I wasn't eating. The waitress would look over at my husband and give him the dirtiest look. If I could read her mind she would be saying something like, "How dare you not allow your wife to eat?" I thought it was pretty funny.

Throughout the months of training for my second competition I still baked mostly cookies and cakes and gave them away. Sometimes I gave my baked goods to the local radio station. I would even hear my name mentioned on the radio thanking me for the goodies. That made my heart happy because it was my way of practicing kindness, and the people were not expecting it. I believe everyone should receive some act of kindness no matter how small.

Two weeks before the competition I was driving, and my children were in the back seat. I was thinking about the competition. There were nine women including me in the bodybuilding competition, three in the lightweight division, three in the middle weight division and three in the heavyweight division. To win overall I would first have to win my weight division and then compete against the other division winners. I suddenly blurted out to my children, "Who wants to carry the small trophy and who wants to carry the big trophy?"

My daughter said, "I want to carry the big one." The strange thing is that I never said that I was going to win. God works in mysterious ways.

There are two parts to the bodybuilding competition, which includes the preliminary competition in the morning and the final round at night. The judges have an overall decision in the morning, and the nighttime competition is basically for show. The winners are not announced until the evening.

To my surprise my father came to the preliminary round of the competition. I was up on the stage in a two-piece posing suit. My father was an old-fashioned man, and I wondered what he thought of me being half naked, although I never asked him. After the show was over my husband asked my father, "How do you think Diana did?"

My father told Roger, "I think she is going to win."

For the first time in my life I felt that my father was proud of me.

The evening competition was more nerve racking than the morning. I was nervous and excited at the same time. The master of ceremonies announced the winners, and he called my name. I won the lightweight division and went on to compete with the other division winners. I beat the other two division winners and won overall. My title was 2002 Ms. Guam National Bodybuilding Champion, and I won a small trophy and a big trophy, four feet tall. Riacca carried the big trophy and Franco carried the small trophy. After I was pronounced the winner, I went backstage. I went up to my trainer, Dave, jumped on him, and wrapped my legs and arms around him. I had never done that to anyone. My level of excitement was beyond what words can explain. I was never so excited in my life to win for the second year. All the hard work and training had paid off. Besides having my children, winning the competition was my biggest accomplishment. I will forever remember that night. It is so amazing that no matter how old I get I will forever have my title. I would have never thought that I would be on a stage in a posing suit flexing my muscles and winning. It all started with my comment of, "Am I too late?"

That night my family, friends, and I went out to celebrate. I ate a chocolate dessert that I had been craving for months, and it tasted so good. The next morning I woke up and my picture along with an article announcing my win was on the back page of the local newspaper. When I saw the picture and article I finally realized that it was real. Several weeks after the competition I had the crazy idea of writing a book titled Am I too late? I thought about it for a while and then got busy with other things that were going on in my life.

Later in that same year I competed in American Samoa and won a silver medal. The people in American Samoa were friendly, and it was beautiful there. The following year I competed in Maui, Hawaii, and won overall. It was super cool because instead of winning a trophy, I won a sword. The last bodybuilding competition I competed in was in the year 2004 in New Zealand. It was my first time in New Zealand, and the island was breathtaking. I did not place, but I still had an amazing time and was able to meet a lot of competitors. In all my competitions I was all natural, with no steroids. Winning isn't everything. It was a great journey for me spiritually, mentally, and physically.

After I returned from New Zealand, some people asked me when I was going to compete again. I was flattered to know that people enjoyed watching me compete. I accomplished my goal of competing, and winning was a bonus, but I wanted to move on to new goals.

Slater achieves her dream

By Yoshitaka Ebisawa
Pacific Daily News
yebisawa@guampdn.com

Since she finished second at the 2001 Sobe Guam Bodybuilding Championships on March 23 last year, becoming Ms. Guam has been Diana Slater's dream.

The 35-year-old athlete has followed a strict diet and workout program since then. On Saturday at Hyatt Regency Guam, all the work Slater put into the Sobe Summer Flex 2002 gave the lightweight what she desired.

"This is something that I worked very hard for for a long time," the 2002 Ms. Guam said a couple of days after the competition. "I feel great. I feel excited, happy, thrilled. This is like a dream come true for me. Dreams do come true."

Having won the contest, Slater's next target will be November's South Pacific Games in Fiji.

"I've never been there, so I want to do my best and try my best," said Slater, who has been in the sport for about 18 months. "So I have to continue my training and my dieting."

Dieting difficult

Slater not only trains at Paradise Fitness Center in Hagåtña, but does cardiovascular exercise outside the gym. But the hardest part is dieting. The mother of two said she ate what she calls lean foods to prepare for the Summer Flex 2002. The foods she eats include chicken without skin; eggs with no yolk; and canned tuna, which she washes before eating.

"It's a very strict diet. You can't have pizza or hamburgers," the world-class athlete said.

but I can't eat them because it's not a part of the bodybuilding diet. ... My goal this year was to win first place overall. In order to reach my goal, I had to work hard and give up the things and foods that I like to eat. You have to dedicate yourself and be very disciplined."

Slater said most women she sees look at her as someone different or someone to admire because of the way she looks.

"I have children, and I take care of my body," said Slater, who weighed 111 pounds on Saturday.

Her husband, Roger Slater, said he has been impressed by his wife's dedication.

"I was very proud of her. In fact, I was cheering so loud that night I almost lost my voice," Roger Slater said. "I don't think most people realize how much work goes into that one competition — you know, the day after day after day. I have huge respect not only for my wife but for all the athletes who were in that competition."

Diana Slater said her desire to win the Ms. Guam title helped her to stay dedicated.

"After the training at the gym, I feel very good," she said. "It's hard to explain. It's hard. It's painful. But after I finish, I feel like I have (come) just one step closer to my goal."

Although she fulfilled her dream to become Ms. Guam, Diana Slater will not retire from the sport.

"My ultimate goal (in bodybuilding) is to go to the Ms. Olympia competition," Slater said. "It's going to be hard because I have to win a world bodybuilding competition to get a professional card to compete in the Ms. Olympia competi-

Masako Watanabe/Pacific Daily News/mwatanabe@guampdn.com
Ms. Guam: Diana Slater poses during Sobe Summer Flex 2002 Saturday at Hyatt Regency Guam. Slater won the Ms. Guam title for 2002.

2002 Ms. Guam National Bodybuilding Champion

Onstage posing for the 2002 Guam National bodybuilding competition

On stage posing for the 2001 Guam National Bodybuilding competition

Backstage warming up for the 2001Guam National bodybuilding competition

Backstage after winning 2002 Ms. Guam National Bodybuilding competition

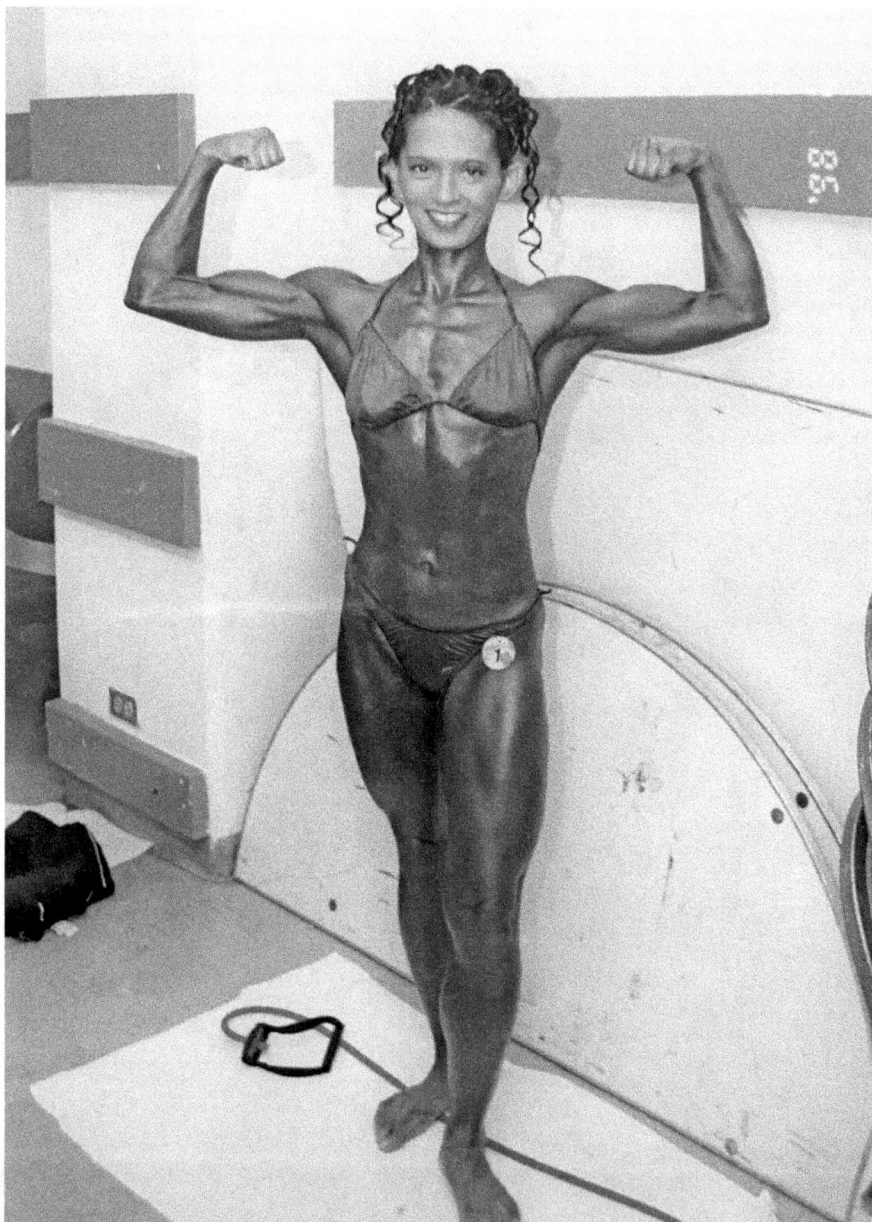

Backstage before the 2002 bodybuilding competition

CHAPTER 7

Life After Competing

I was a personal trainer for a few years after competing, and I really enjoyed it. It was great meeting new people, helping them set their goals, and seeing positive results. I had a few clients ask me to put together a healthy meal plan for them, and I was happy to help. I asked them to write down what they consumed in a typical day, including anything they drank. I explained to them that I would be able to give them a list of healthy choices, but I was not a dietitian.

One afternoon Roger, the children, and I decided to go to the movies. While Roger was in the process of parking my car on the side of the movie theater, I stated, "I don't think you should park there. The car might get stolen."No other cars were parked where Roger parked. Sure enough, we got out of the movie at three o'clock in the afternoon, and the car was gone. I was shocked that in broad daylight someone would actually steal my car. I felt violated. The next day Roger took his car and drove around an area where my car was stolen to see if he could find it. Roger located my car parked near the area of other movie theaters. He called the police, and they arrived a few minutes later. Surprisingly the only damage to my car was a small hole through the door lock on the front passenger side. At that moment I realized that I parked my car at the airport and placed the spare key in the ashtray weeks before I went on a trip. I totally forgot the spare key was still in the ashtray, and that was how the individual or individuals were able to steal the car. I was very grateful the damage to my car was minor. Life is like a road. Sometimes it is smooth and things are going great and sometimes we experience small bumps or potholes, and we sort through our problems and move on with life. I thank God when good things happen and pray to get through the rough times.

After we got married we were renting a house and decided it was time to purchase a home. In the year 2004 we started looking around for a new home, and we looked at several houses. Some of the houses we looked at needed work, and I wanted a house that was move-in ready. We finally agreed on a house, purchased it, and moved in January 2005. It was beautiful, and I called it country living. It was in an area of the island that was less populated and had heavy vegetation around the house.

I occasionally saw deer, wild boar, snakes, spiders, and iguanas near the house. The first time I saw deer up close it was a family, and it was beautiful. Every single time I saw a deer it was breathtaking. It always made my day when I saw a deer. The snakes were not poisonous. I learned how to use my machete to kill snakes. I did not approach the wild boars, because they are very dangerous. The spiders were banana spiders, and they lived outdoors. They were hairy, did not form a web, and they jumped. I was told that they were not poisonous, but I didn't want to find out. I usually kept several cans of Black Flag long-range bug spray to kill the spiders. I saw spiders several times during the year. The spiders scared me the most. The times that I saw iguanas, they ran away if I approached them. There were also stray chickens that came around every day, most especially after I started feeding them. One particular chicken that I named Henry waited on my porch for me every day and followed me around my yard.

I had a great time connecting with nature.

By the time we lived in our new house we had seven cats. I always said they found me. All the cats got along, with the exception of Sabrina. For some reason she didn't care to associate with the other cats. The most recent cat I found in the beach parking lot was a two-week-old kitten. I bottle-fed him, and since then he followed me around as if I were his mommy. Basically I was the only mom that he knew. His name was Flash. All our cats died of old age with the exception of two. Caramel had diabetes, and Sammy got outside and was hit by a car. Cupid was depressed after Sammy died.

I then figured I should get a dog for my husband. My husband named him Zeus. When we first brought Zeus home all of the cats were afraid of him except for Flash. As time passed all the cats learned to tolerate Zeus. I enjoyed many years with all the animals, but when they each died I felt like there was a hole in my heart.

A few years later our house was burglarized. I came home in the middle of the afternoon, opened the front door, and I noticed the house was a complete mess. I walked around the house and noticed a big hole in a bedroom window with a concrete block inside the room. I felt violated and afraid once again. First my car was stolen and now our house was burglarized. A lot of our personal belongings were stolen, including a bracelet that my mother had given me. I wanted to pass that bracelet down to my daughter. I know things can be replaced and not people, and I was grateful that that no harm was done to my family. We called the police and officers arrived sometime later. I provided the police with a list of items stolen, but the police never recovered any of our items. For several weeks I couldn't sleep throughout the night. Anytime I heard any noise I jumped up and was afraid once again. Not even a year later the house was burglarized again. I came home in the afternoon and it was like déjàvu. It seemed like whatever wasn't stolen the first time was stolen the second time around. I felt violated all over again, but I was very grateful that my family was not hurt. After we were burglarized twice my husband and I decided it was time to get a security system installed. Once the security system was installed I felt better and was finally able to sleep through the night.

CHAPTER **8**

Police Department

I ALWAYS ENJOYED watching law enforcement television shows, most especially *Law and Order*. I would envision myself as a female detective on the television show. During the summer of 2009 I decided to enroll in a six-week supplemental Police Academy at the community college. My first day at the community college, the entire class was introduced to the cadre. The cadre is a police officer in charge of the physical fitness training portion of the supplemental academy. The cadre told us if the class couldn't take criticism from him then we wouldn't be able to handle what the public had in store for us. The cadre yelled at the class every day. The first time the cadre yelled, I said to myself, "What am I doing? I am in my forties, and I don't like getting yelled at. What am I trying to prove?" As time passed I learned not to take the yelling personally and just let it go in one ear and out the other. I focused on my goal, which was to pass the supplemental academy and apply for the police department. The cadre made the class participants run, do sit-ups and push-ups daily. There was also an obstacle course, which included flipping massive tires from one side to the other. I needed the help of two of my classmates to flip the tires.

The class also had classroom time with instructors that were also police officers. The classroom instruction was a variety of basic law

Police Officer at Hagatna Precinct

enforcement classes, but in a condensed version. At first it was difficult for me to focus on schoolwork because it had been many years since I had to study, but eventually I was able to get it. Although it was a very challenging six weeks, I made it through the supplemental academy. It felt great to accomplish my goal. I was also the oldest person in the class. I was also the only person to graduate from the supplemental academy who did eventually go to work for the police department.

The last day of class one of the instructors informed the class that the local police department was hiring police officers. I was excited, and I went to put in my application. I took the written test in August 2009 and passed. By the summer of 2010 I was beginning to lose hope, because I hadn't heard anything from the police department. I finally received a phone call in July 2010 and the individual on the other line asked if I was still interested in becoming a police officer. I said yes. I had to pass a timed obstacle course, polygraph test, and finally meet with the interview board, which was a panel of several police officers. I was extremely nervous meeting with the interview board. I passed all the tests and started the police academy in December 2010. The first day of the academy I was full of nerves and excitement at the same time. The police academy was six months long and included both physical fitness and classroom time. All the instructors were police officers. The six months were filled with physical and mental stress; however, I had a goal in sight and nothing was going to stop me.

One day the class had physical fitness and was running around the police department headquarters. I was stopped by a high-ranking officer who stated, "Slater, aren't you a little too old to be doing this?"

I responded, "Sir, I will leave my classmates in the dust."

He laughed and walked away.

Because the class spent so much time together, we bonded. I was the oldest, and the class nicknamed me Jesus's Mother. It didn't bother me, because I was proud of myself. I realized sometime after I turned thirty years old that with the help of God, once I set my mind to doing something, no matter how hard it is, I just do it.

While I was with the class practicing shooting on the firing range, a reporter from the local newspaper found out that I was the oldest one in the academy and wanted to interview me. The article and picture of me was published on the front page on Mother's Day 2011. I was super excited. It was amazing. I made the back of the local newspaper in the year 2002 and the front page on 2011.

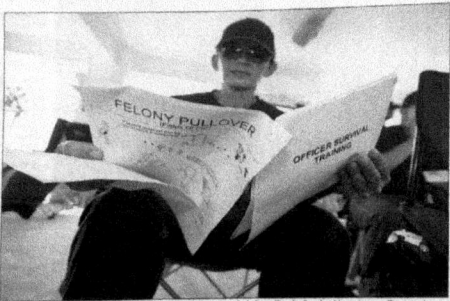

Pacific Sunday News

Charter school seeks $4M

Guåhan Academy awaits board's budget approval

Mom takes on new challenge

Police Academy at age 44

48

After I graduated from the police academy it took me a few days to realize it was real. For several weeks I was assigned to a field training officer, called an FTO, who had to go on every call with me. I really enjoyed being a police officer, except for the times when the situation was very stressful and I would have nightmares for several weeks. I spent several years on patrol and one year as a detective in the Domestic Violence/Criminal Sexual Conduct Unit. I found my niche when I was a detective. I interviewed countless victims and arrested suspects. As a victim of sexual assault and family violence myself, I felt that I was able to better understand the victims. I was also able to have closure in my personal life.

After several months as a police officer, on one of my off days I was shopping at the grocery store and was approached by a female adult. She introduced herself and stated, "After I read your newspaper article on Mother's Day I was so inspired by you that I went back to college." I thanked her and told her I was extremely flattered. It was one of the nicest compliments I have ever received in my life.

As a police officer I continued to practice kindness. On several occasions I baked cookies, monkey bread, and banana bread for my fellow police officers. I also cooked turkey chili and turkey balls for my coworkers. They were very appreciative and it made me happy too.

On one occasion as I was grocery shopping on my day off from work and I was approached by an elderly man pushing a shopping cart. The man told me he didn't have enough money to pay for his groceries and asked me if I could pay for his groceries. I gladly said yes, and we proceeded to the cashier line. I told the cashier I would be paying for his groceries and to please ring up his groceries first. The man thanked me, and my heart was extremely happy. Every single time I practiced kindness my heart skipped a beat and it made my day. Several months later I saw the same man, but it was not on good circumstances. I was on duty and responded to an expired-person call. I arrived at a residence and found the man had died alone in his house. I took one look at him and instantly remembered him at the grocery store and started to cry. It was an extremely sad day for me; however, I will always remember his smile when I paid for his groceries.

On another occasion I was shopping at Kmart on my day off from work, and once again was approached by an elderly man pushing a grocery cart. The man told me he didn't have enough money and asked me if I could pay for his groceries. I gladly said yes, and we proceeded to the cashier line. I told the cashier I would be paying for his groceries as well as my groceries. The man thanked me, and once again my heart was extremely happy.

I am not sure why the two men approached me and asked me, but I am very thankful that I was able to help. I always remember where I came from, and I hope that I can always be able to practice kindness. I wished the world had more kind people. There is no such thing as only a small act of kindness.

After my first year as a police officer my plan was to stay in the police department and retire in twenty years. The police department is very political and things didn't go the way I had planned. I wanted to stay as a detective, but a higher ranking police officer didn't think I was fit for that department anymore, so I was transferred back to patrol. I started having doubts about my abilities as a police officer and I wasn't good enough to stay as a detective, which led to me getting depressed. I was transferred to a precinct in a village where the crime was extremely bad. I prayed a lot to help me get through all the stress. I was thinking about putting in my resignation.

The police department had a small group of volunteer police officers. I met James, who was one of the volunteers who worked on my shift for a couple of days. On his second day of my shift James and I were talking, and I mentioned that I was looking for another job. James went on to say that he worked at the Federal Courthouse and it was hiring. James wrote down his supervisor's name, Pete, and cell phone number, and said it would be okay to call him. I called Pete the next day, and he asked me to come in for an interview. After the interview Pete made me a conditional offer. He stated I would first have to pass a federal background check, and I agreed. After several months Pete called to inform me that my background was good and asked when I would be able to start. I was very excited about the news and told him my start date.

I gave my two-week resignation notice. My last day in the police department was a sad day for me, not only because I knew I would miss police work but also because only one of my coworkers wished me luck.

CHAPTER 9

Court Security Officer

IN APRIL 2016 I started as a court security officer contracted under the United States Marshal Service at the Federal Courthouse in Guam. It was a great job with the weekends off. Court security officers stand post at several locations throughout the courthouse. The job also included operating x-ray machines and scanning and distributing mail. My coworkers and I got along, or at least I thought we all did. Most of my coworkers had been retired or were former law enforcement officers. I formed a bond with the maintenance employees at the court. There were two cleaning women, Tess and Belin, who were responsible for cleaning the courthouse and two men, Ramon and Vic, in maintenance. After some time Belin left Guam for Wyoming and Cherry became the new cleaning woman. I got to know Tess, Belin, and Cherry, including their birthdays. To me birthdays are very special, and I gave money to all three women and two maintenance men for their birthdays. They were surprised and happy, which in turn made me happy too. I told Tess, Belin, and Cherry that I give out of the kindness of my heart and never expect anything in return. True giving is from the heart. Cherry had a young daughter, Eunice, and I asked Cherry when her daughter's birthday was. We talked about what Eunice liked, and Cherry told me that she liked the movie Frozen. I bought a doll that mimicked a character from the movie Frozen to give to Eunice as her birthday gift. Cherry was so happy and

I was too. I remember where I came from, and I am fortunate to be able to practice kindness. All three women always gave me a birthday gift. I was always surprised and very grateful.

One of my coworkers, Joe, told me a story about when he was a police officer. Joe had a supervisor in the police department who always told him to make coffee for him. Joe said one day he was so tired of making coffee that he used toilet water to make his supervisor's coffee to get revenge. I thought that was evil and wondered how anyone could do something so mean.

One day one of the posts at work was not staffed at the scheduled time. I mentioned to the person in charge that Joe wasn't at his post and I also asked him not to mention my name. If one of the marshals found out, all the court security officers would get written up, so I was afraid. I was trying to look out for all of us. Joe took it the wrong way and was angry with me. I apologized to Joe, but he did not accept my apology. He instead reminded me of the toilet water story. As soon as Joe said that, I remembered that morning I made coffee and noticed that the water level was low in the coffeemaker. Joe never came right out and admitted that he put toilet water in the coffeemaker, but he insinuated it. I felt disgusted. I would never have thought anyone could hate me so much as to try to poison me. After that incident happened I informed my supervisor that I needed to take off one week from work to pray on it and figure things out. During my week off I talked to a priest, and it felt as if a huge weight was lifted off my shoulders. I prayed and decided to go back to work to prove to my coworker that I was the better person.

I know God is with me always.

The following week I returned to work and was my joyful self. Several weeks later Joe apologized to me and asked me if we could start over. I accepted his apology, and we shook hands.

I continued to stay active, mostly jogging. During the weekdays I jogged on my treadmill at home. On the weekends I went on long jogs, sometimes up to eight miles. I felt an endorphin high after I finished each long jog. One year I competed in a half marathon, and two years later I competed in a marathon. My goal was to finish the race and not be last. Because I am not a fast runner I knew I wasn't going to finish first, but I have endurance.

In the latter part of 2017 I reconnected with my first cousin Roland. He invited me to a family Thanksgiving gathering, and I accepted his invitation. At that time Roger was working overseas, so I went alone. I had a great time and I thanked Roland for inviting me. I had an instant connection with Roland. I felt like I was able to talk to him about anything that was going on in my life. For the next several months we spent almost every Saturday having dinner, and it was great. Roland mentioned that he had met the pope years earlier. I know it may sound strange but it made me feel closer to God. In the month of October Roland sent me a text message that it was the month of the rosary. It is because of Roland that I pray the rosary every day. I also pray the Devine Mercy right after the rosary. I know God brought Roland into my life, and I will be forever grateful.

In the latter part of February 2018 my husband had back surgery. A few days later he fell into a coma and was on a breathing ventilator. I had never been so frightened for him and for the family. The doctors said he had an infection in his back that had traveled to his brain. The doctor informed the family that a tracheal tube would be inserted to help him breathe and a feeding tube would be inserted in his stomach. The doctors also talked about long-term care. They mentioned that Guam did not have a facility and we would have to travel to the States. I had a hard time grasping everything that happened to my husband and was in tears. I went home, cried, and prayed. God heard my prayer, because the next day Roger woke up from his coma. He spent a total of five weeks in the hospital before he was able to go home. He had to relearn to feed himself, walk, and bathe himself. The neurologist said he might never regain his short-term memory as a result of the damage from the infection. After Roger was released from the hospital I stayed home with him for several weeks before I returned to work. I wanted to make sure that he would be okay at home by himself. Eventually he was able to drive again, which made him happy too. Roger looked like the same person, but his short-term memory was bad and he did not show any emotion. When something that was sad happened and I was crying, he didn't comfort me. If I was upset at him for something he did, he didn't apologize. The old Roger was a considerate person, but now a lot of times he is selfish. The incident in the hospital changed Roger. I told myself to pray extra prayers every day to accept the new Roger and not blame him, because he is not the same person he was before the surgery. Most days I am patient with Roger because God is by my side.

I mentioned to Roger that when I turn fifty-five years old I want to sell our house and relocate to the States. He thought it was a great idea. We talked about moving to Texas or Alabama. We wanted to move someplace that was cold during winter but not have to shovel snow.

CHAPTER 10

COVID-19

EARLY IN THE year 2020 Covid-19 came out of a lab in China and then spread all over the world because Chinese people were traveling. The world was pretty much at a standstill. On Guam only essential workers went to work, which included hospitals, supermarkets, and gas stations that were opened. Schools were closed. Everyplace of business required people to wear masks to be able to go inside. My hours at work were cut to two or three days a week. I had a lot of time on my hands. I was praying the rosary, Devine Mercy, and listening to the Bible in a Year every day. I did some painting around the house, which I found therapeutic. I spent some time on YouTube and discovered some random act of kindness videos. These videos helped me feel happy to see people going out of their way to be kind to other people. I started appreciating the small things in life and having positive thinking. In late 2020 I was back to working full time at my job, but we still had to wear masks. There were a couple of my coworkers that I had grown fond of, namely Pat and Roland. They were always good to me. Pat had a great sense of humor, and he always made me smile.

CHAPTER 11

Practicing Kindness on Guam

I HAVE BEEN practicing kindness for many years. I not only enjoyed baking, but it also was my stress reliever. Sometime after Roger and I got married he had a small business that included a partner. I found a recipe for snickerdoodle cookies, and my family loved them. It was the holiday season, and I thought that instead of giving out fruit baskets to Roger's clients I would bake snickerdoodle cookies and give them to his clients instead. His clients loved the cookies so much that years later they still remembered me baking snickerdoodles for them. Seeing joy in the faces of people after they had my cookies made me feel happy too.

When I was competing in bodybuilding, on multiple occasions I baked various types of cookies, and after they cooled I wrapped them in cellophane and gave them away to the local radio station. The radio announcer often thanked me on the air. I was flattered. I always practice kindness out of the goodness of my heart and never for an ulterior motive. One day I was delivering cookies to the radio station and one of the radio staff members was in the elevator with me. He asked me if I was the person who made the cookies, and I said yes. He responded with, "This whole time I always thought it was a little old lady that made the cookies." He made me chuckle.

When I was in the police academy I baked monkey bread and cookies and brought them to class. The class was appreciative. Even after I became a police officer I baked chocolate chip cookies and banana bread and brought those things to work for my fellow police officers. On different occasions I also made turkey chili and turkey balls and brought them to work.

I got the idea of practicing kindness at the grocery store incident during Covid-19, and I was watching the YouTube videos of random acts of kindness. I did not video any of my acts of kindness because I just wanted to do something nice. I went grocery shopping, and I decided to practice kindness. At first I would observe people and see what kinds of items were in their grocery cart. I chose mostly elderly people, because I figured they would be on a fixed income, plus groceries are expensive on Guam. I walked up to the people I chose and told them I was practicing kindness and asked them if it was okay if I paid for their groceries. The people I approached were always very thankful and full of smiles. It made me extremely happy, and sometimes it felt like my heart was dancing. I am a very fortunate person and I remember where I came from. I practiced acts of kindness at the grocery store often. One Christmas I won $500.00 worth of gift certificates for the grocery store, and instead of using them for my groceries I decided to give it away. Every week I gave away one $50.00 gift certificate at the grocery store to a random customer, mostly the elderly. There were two separate occasions when the women cried after I told them I was practicing kindness and gave them the gift certificates. It really touched my heart, and I was very grateful I was able to help them. Even after I gave all the gift certificates away I continued to practice kindness at the grocery store.

Another way I practiced kindness was when I went to a drive-through at a fast food restaurant. I ordered my food at the drive-through and then went to the window to pay. I asked the cashier how much the bill was for the car behind me, and I told the cashier to add their bill together with mine. I usually got a smile or look of confusion from the cashier. I would tell the cashier, "If they ask just tell them I was practicing kindness."

My house was a quarter of a mile from the nearest gas station. I got to know most of the employees at the gas station and formed a bond with Jen. Jen was a single mother with two beautiful children. I occasionally baked cookies or banana bread and brought them for the employees at the gas station. It brought a smile to them, and it made my day. On several occasions on my day off from work I went to the gas station and observed people. I would approach elderly people with older cars, tell them I was practicing kindness, and ask if it was okay if I paid for their gas. All the smiles I received were priceless, and the people were always thankful. I always smiled back and said, "You're welcome."

There were a few times when I was at the gas station and wasn't able to find the right person. I would ask Jen if it was okay if I left her the money and she could choose the right person for me. Jen was happy to help execute my acts of kindness. I trusted her. The different stories were priceless that Jen shared with me after she was a helper in practicing kindness. One of the stories was that a young woman with an older car walked into the gas station and placed a handful of coins on the counter. The young woman stated she would like to buy gas for her car, which Jen acknowledged. Jen did not tell the young mother about the extra money she would be adding to gas up her car. A few minutes later the young woman walked back inside the gas station and told Jen there was a mistake with her gas. Jen told her that there was no mistake and that a woman practicing kindness paid for her gas. The young woman cried and told Jen that she had just lost her job. She also told Jen that instead of dropping her son at the bus stop, she could drive him to school. After Jen told me the reaction of the young mother, I cried.

The gas station had a soft-serve ice cream machine. On several occasions I paid for thirteen ice cream cones and asked Jen to please pick thirteen people to give the ice cream cones to. Jen was always happy to help. Jen told me she usually picked children, and they were always extremely happy to have free ice cream. One Mother's Day I bought thirteen ice cream cones and Jen gave them away to mothers. I thanked Jen for helping me, because most times mothers don't feel appreciated. I am very grateful to have met Jen and her beautiful children. Jen is a wonderful woman.

I also became friends with one of the gas attendants named Val. Val was always very helpful, whether it be to fill my tank with gasoline, fill my tires with air, or clean my windshield. I thanked Val for his help and often tipped him. On one occasion I saw a young girl in the gas station with Val, and he introduced me to his daughter. That Christmas I bought a gift for Val's young daughter, and she was very thankful. It made me happy because she was happy. Val told me that he had never met anyone like me. I told him that was one of the nicest compliments I had ever received.

In the latter part of 2021 we went to Texas to visit Riacca. While we were in Texas we stayed with Riacca. Roger and I decided that we wanted to relocate to Texas and wanted to meet with a real estate agent to see what the housing market was like. The real estate agent showed us a few houses. We informed him that we would not be buying right away, but as soon as we sold our house on Guam we would contact him. We were excited about moving to Texas.

Even though we were on vacation, I continued to go jogging. Riacca showed me an area that was safe to jog near her condo. For the next several days I went jogging, usually before the sun came up. One morning I was jogging and did not see a skunk until it was too late. I screamed and the skunk sprayed me. I had to throw away most of my clothes and shoes. I heard stories that once a skunk sprays people they have to shower multiple times to get the stink out. Thank God I had to shower only once. Riacca felt bad that I was sprayed and my son-in-law jokingly asked if I was trying to pet the skunk. He knows that I am an animal lover, but I know not to get near a skunk. Aside from the skunk incident I had a great time.

We flew back to Guam and met with a real estate agent to sell our house on Guam. We had a great meeting. We discussed and decided on the selling price. The agent took pictures of the house and placed the house on the market. We had several families come and look at the house within a short period of time. Two families put in a bid. The house sold in less than a month, and we were very happy.

When I put the house up for sale I had told Jen and Val, and they were surprised that I was leaving Guam. They both said that they would miss me. Jen told me that she had never met anyone like me before. I thanked her for making my day. I told them that I would miss them too. Jen told me that when we sold the house she would come over and help me pack. I was very appreciative. Jen asked to buy my car. I told Jen that my car had a lot of problems, but if she still wanted to buy it, I would sell it to her.

Val told me that he and his wife needed a new bed and asked if I had one for sale. I told Val I would give him the bed if he would help me with packing when the house sold, and he was very happy to help. Early March 2022 was when the movers came to the house to pack up our belongings. Both Jen and Val showed up at the house to help me, and I was very grateful. Roger and I didn't take all of our personal belongings when we left Guam. We sold some of our personal items, and we gave away a lot. Because Jen and Val stayed and helped me out all day, I gave a lot of personal belongings to them. Jen bought my car. That day was bittersweet for me. I was happy to be starting a new chapter of my life, but I would miss all the kind people I met, to include Jen and Val. The day before I left Guam I went to say my goodbyes to the gas-station personnel, especially Jen and Val. Jen gave me a huge hug and told me she would miss me. I was crying and told her I would never forget her. I said goodbye to Val, and he was crying. I told him I would miss him. I never had a man cry for me, with the exception of my husband. I didn't have the opportunity to say goodbye to my best friend Cathy. Cathy and I had many adventures together and I will definitely miss that. Our belief in prayers and God is also very strong. I was hopeful that when I got to Texas I was going to be able to practice kindness and meet more exceptional people.

CHAPTER 12

Texas

I WAS HOMESICK during my first several months in Texas. I even had doubts about selling the house in Guam and moving to Texas. I missed the people and I missed practicing kindness. Every single time I practiced kindness on Guam everyone was very receptive. After a couple of weeks I decided to practice kindness at the grocery store to help me snap out of being sad. I was in line at the grocery store to pay for my groceries. I approached an elderly woman who was in line behind me and told her I was practicing kindness and asked her if it be okay if I paid for her groceries. She looked right at me and said, "I can pay for my own groceries." I was dumbfounded and didn't know what to say. That was the first time I was shut down trying to practice kindness.

I realized that Texas was nothing like Guam, and I started to feel like I didn't belong. I prayed more than usual, started listening to Christian music, and meditated. Listening to Christian music helped me realize that God is the only one that is there for me, no matter what the circumstance. My daughter once told me that God won't give us more than I can handle. She is absolutely right. Once again I focused on appreciating the small things in life, like the sunshine and the birds singing. I told myself I would find other ways to practice kindness. There is no such thing as a small act of kindness. Somewhere along the line I realized even if it is my plan, if it is not God's plan, it won't happen. I believe with God anything is possible; you just have to believe.

When we moved to Texas my initial plan was to apply for a job at the airlines, but I decided to try working in loss prevention. During the month of May 2022 I had three job interviews with three different companies. I received one job offer that was not my first choice, but I was grateful. I started my job as a loss prevention officer for a hotel. Mostly everyone who worked at the hotel were nice people, but it still took me several months before I felt like I fit in.

Even though I fit in at the hotel I decided to see a therapist to help me with my unresolved issues that I had been dealing with for so many years. I had less than ten sessions with the therapist, but she really helped me. I shared with my therapist the sexual abuse, emotional abuse, and physical abuse I had been through. She helped me learn to forgive the people who had done me wrong, learn to heal, and to focus on making new goals. Forgiveness was a huge weight lifted from my shoulders. I told my therapist the time when I won the bodybuilding competition, and I had this crazy idea to write a book and title it Am I too late? She said, "Why don't you write a book?"If it weren't for her encouragement I wouldn't be writing this book. Since I have been writing my book it has also helped me with healing. I ask God everyday to help me to continue to write.

One day I was at work talking with one of the women and telling her that I always have to pray for patience with my husband. She shared a story with me about being married. She told me that she had been married for forty years, and when an argument started with her husband she just walked away and said to him, "I am going to heaven."I told her I loved that and I would use that. The very next time my husband made me angry I just walked away and said to him, "I am going to heaven. I am going to heaven." It worked. I was not angry anymore, and I was happy. I have gotten a lot better with patience with my husband. I do truly hope one day I get to go to heaven.

To me birthdays are special, and when I get to know a person I find out when their birthday is. In my opinion the housekeepers and dishwashers are the hardest working people in the hotel. Most of the employees in the housekeeping department mostly speak Spanish. I downloaded an application on my cell phone to help me learn to speak Spanish and have learned to speak some words. I have gotten to know all the housekeepers by name, and I ask them about their birthdays. When it came time for their birthday I wished them happy birthday and gave them money. They were always most appreciative and always gave me a hug. On my birthday in September 2022 I have never felt so much love. The housekeepers gave me a cake, balloons, flowers, and gifts. It made me cry. When I give I always give from my heart and never expect anything in return, because to me that is the meaning of true giving.

During the month of September 2022 there was a step challenge at work, and I joined, even though I started several days late. I figured because I started late and was several thousands of steps behind I would not catch up to the person in first place. As the weeks passed the people at work asked me how I was able to walk more than 40,000 steps a day. I said, "I just decided I was going to do it, and I did." I also explained that I was a person who, once my mind is made up to doing a task no matter how difficult, I just decide I am going to do it. The month ended and I walked more than 1,100,000 steps and won the step challenge. I used the prize money to buy doughnuts and pizza for the housekeeping department. I know it was only a step challenge, but to me it was another thing that I had accomplished. I believe everyone should always be proud of themselves no matter how small the accomplishment.

I continue to practice kindness by baking cookies and cakes and giving them to the employees at the hotel. Occasionally I practice random acts of kindness by giving the dishwashers some money. I have also baked cookies and banana bread for the Little Elm Senior Citizens Center.

During the month of December 2022 my place of work was accepting toy donations for children attending a preschool near the hotel. I thought about what toys would be nice to donate, and I decided it would be great to give a girl's bicycle and a boy's bicycle. The day I brought the bicycles into work I was told that nobody had ever donated bicycles in the past. I was really surprised. I just wanted to buy something nice for the children, and I always enjoy practicing kindness. Christmas is my favorite holiday, and I always enjoy giving, especially when it is least expected.

CHAPTER 13

Conclusion

I TREAT PEOPLE the way I would like to be treated. I smile at people and tell them to have a nice day. Every morning I wake up and am grateful for a good night's sleep and for the ability to live another day. I enjoy today, because tomorrow is not a guarantee. I stay positive. Happiness starts from within. If you are not happy with yourself you can't make other people happy. God willing, I will be able to practice kindness for the rest of my life. Learn to appreciate even the smallest things in life, like the sunshine and the birds. Joy is a choice, just like love. If I could have one wish I would wish the world had more kind people.

I wrote this book in hopes to inspire someone. Despite all the obstacles I had early in life, I did not let them stop me from accomplishing whatever goal I had at the time. Looking back now, every time I felt overwhelmed, cried, and prayed to God, he never failed me. From the bodybuilding competitions in my thirties, police officer in my forties, running a half marathon and marathon in my fifties, and now writing a book, there is no impossible. I believe if you want to accomplish anything, as long as you set your mind to it and are not afraid of hard work, you can do it. I also believe everyone has that same drive and determination in them, and they just have to find that passion. The key is to believe in yourself and have faith.

www.ingramcontent.com/pod-product-compliance
Lightning Source LLC
Chambersburg PA
CBHW051433090426
42737CB00014B/2960